D1483312

RICK YANCEY

RICK YANCEY

LISA WADE McCORMICK

ROSEN
PUBLISHING®

New York

Published in 2014 by The Rosen Publishing Group, Inc.
29 East 21st Street, New York, NY 10010

Copyright © 2014 by The Rosen Publishing Group, Inc.

First Edition

Library of Congress Cataloging-in-Publication Data

McCormick, Lisa Wade, 1961–
Rick Yancey/Lisa Wade McCormick.—First edition.
    pages cm.—(All About the Author)
Includes bibliographical references and index.
ISBN 978-1-4777-1767-7 (library binding)
1. Yancey, Richard—Juvenile literature. 2. Authors,
American—21st century—Biography—Juvenile literature.
I. Title.
PS3625.A675Z75 2014
813'.6—dc23
[B]
                                        2013013958

Manufactured in the United States of America

CPSIA Compliance Information: Batch #W14YA: For further information, contact Rosen Publishing,
New York, New York, at 1-800-237-9932.

CONTENTS

Author Rick Yancey inspired a generation of young readers when he penned eleven simple words: "I never thought I'd save the world—or die saving it." This is the opening line in Yancey's best-selling book for young adults, *The Extraordinary Adventures of Alfred Kropp*. These words convinced thousands of reluctant readers, especially boys, to turn off their video games and read electrifying tales about a secret order of knights, international spies, and an awkward teenager who saves the day.

"I've had an enormous reaction from parents who said they could never get their sons to read and now they can't get them to put down my books to go to bed," Yancey told the *Gainesville Sun* newspaper.

The award-winning author became an instant hero to middle grade students in 2005 when *The Extraordinary Adventures of Alfred Kropp* arrived in bookstores nationwide. The action-packed saga follows a fifteen-year-old "oversized underachiever" who is duped into stealing King Arthur's legendary sword, Excalibur. The young hero's journey continues in the next books in Yancey's swashbuckling trilogy: *The Seal of Solomon* (2007) and *The Thirteenth Skull* (2008).

Yancey's series received high praise from librarians and captured top honors in children's

Author Rick Yancey inspired children around the world to read with his action-packed books that feature unexpected heroes, bloody sword fights, gruesome monsters, and aliens invading Earth.

publishing. *The Extraordinary Adventures of Alfred Kropp* earned a coveted spot on *Publishers Weekly's* "Best Books of 2005" list and was nominated for the prestigious Carnegie Medal. Warner Brothers Pictures also bought the movie rights for the story inspired by the legendary tales of King Arthur and the Knights of the Round Table.

Yancey scared the wits out of readers with his second spellbinding series for young adults. The chilling *Monstrumologist* series takes readers inside the haunting world of a twelve-year-old orphan who helps a scientist track headless, flesh-eating monsters and other creatures of the night. Yancey weaves his terrifying tale through four frightening books: *The Monstrumologist* (2009), *The Curse of the Wendigo* (2010), *The Isle of Blood* (2011), and *The Final Descent* (2013).

Some reviewers and librarians criticized the blood and gore in Yancey's grisly series. But many others, such as *VOYA*, applauded it for delivering "nightmares in a literary package." *The Monstrumologist* won the 2010 Michael L. Printz Award, which honors the best book written for teens.

Yancey switched from bloodthirsty monsters to deadly aliens in his third series for young readers, a trilogy that starts with the book *The 5th Wave*. The

5th Wave, released in 2013, mixes romance with danger in the story of a teenage girl who tries to rescue her brother after extraterrestrials invade Earth. Can she trust the mysterious stranger who offers to help save her brother? Or is he an alien disguised as a human?

Putnam Books for Young Readers reportedly paid seven figures for rights to the highly touted series, which marked the first time Yancey has ventured into the world of science fiction. Hollywood also snatched up the movie rights to this alien invasion masterpiece.

What adventures lie ahead for Yancey and his legion of devoted fans? Don't be surprised if this master storyteller—who also writes novels and mysteries for adults—takes young readers on more heart-pounding, page-turning adventures filled with unsavory characters, unthinkable monsters, unmerciful aliens, and unlikely heroes who save the day.

CHAPTER ONE

CHASING HIS WRITING DREAM

T he first chapters in Rick Yancey's life aren't filled with heroic battles to save the world or close encounters with aliens. The early pages of this best-selling author's story aren't nearly as exciting as the tales he weaves in his internationally acclaimed books. But his story has a nerdy kid who becomes a hero to millions of young readers—and gets the girl of his dreams.

YANCEY'S OPENING CHAPTER

Yancey's story began on a balmy Sunday in Florida. He was born on November 4, 1962, in Miami. In an

Rick Yancey's father, Quillian S. Yancey, is sworn in as interim sheriff of Polk County, Florida, in 1976. Quillian Yancey was a respected attorney and longtime Florida politician.

interview with the Web site Dread Central, Yancey said he was "adopted and raised in central Florida by the son of a sharecropper turned attorney."

The celebrated author grew up in an upper-middle-class family in Lakeland, Florida. His father, Quillian S. Yancey, was an attorney, a former agent with the Federal Bureau of Investigation (FBI), and a longtime Florida politician. The southern gentleman—and son of a poor Georgia share-cropper—served as Florida's state attorney, state representative, and state senator during his forty-year career in public service.

Quillian Yancey was known for his character-istic Stetson hat, no-nonsense attitude, and the use of colorful phrases such as "by cracky." He died on January 3, 2005. Yancey's mother, Norma, was a legal secretary and active member of her church. She died on March 1, 2007. Yancey has two siblings—an older brother, Jay, and a younger sister, Lynn.

As a boy, Yancey was a shy, awkward kid with "moplike bushy hair and glasses," he said in an interview with Bloomsbury Children's Publishing. "Growing up, I often felt like an outcast, kind of a loner."

Yancey, however, has fond memories of the lazy summer days he spent at his grandmother's house in Homeland, Florida. "My grandmother lived in a typical Florida house with a big screened-in porch, and she had a huge yard and a big field that we played in," he told the *Ledger* newspaper.

Yancey found many adventures on the pages of mysteries, science fiction, and fantasy novels. "My parents always encouraged me to read," he wrote on his Web site, RickYancey.com.

One of his favorite childhood books was Roald Dahl's *Charlie and the Chocolate Factory*. "Love the humor," he told the Web site BookBrowse.com. Other authors who inspired Yancey's young imagination were Terry Brooks (*The Sword of Shannara*), Arthur Conan Doyle (*The Adventures of Sherlock Holmes*), and J. R. R. Tolkien (*The Hobbit*).

FORESHADOWING HIS FUTURE

Yancey started writing his own stories in fifth grade. Three years later, when he was a junior high school student, Yancey penned a story that foreshadowed his future as an author. "I had an assignment in language arts class to write a five-page narrative short story," Yancey told the *Ledger*. "We were studying stories of survival and we had to write a story around that theme."

Something suddenly clicked. Yancey's imagination ran wild. Words flowed onto the page. He ended up with a twenty-five-page saga about a man lost

Rick Yancey graduated from Roosevelt University in Chicago, Illinois, with a degree in English. He attended law school for one year and worked several unusual jobs before he became a full-time writer.

in the swamp. "That was my first clue that writing might be for me," Yancey said.

The budding author was fourteen years old when he wrote that tale, which changed the course of his life. His teacher's reaction to the story also fueled his dream to become a writer. "I wrote a note to him, apologizing for the length, and he wrote back, 'Never apologize for something you should be proud of,'" Yancey told blogger Vivian Lee Mahoney. "That note always stuck with me."

Yancey's first published story appeared in the Lakeland High School literary magazine. The story was about a Native American whose child dies in infancy.

PLOT TWISTS

Yancey continued to chase his writing dream after high school. He attended Florida Southern College in Lakewood, transferred to Florida State University in Tallahassee, and later graduated from Roosevelt University in Chicago with a degree in English.

Yancey, however, didn't immediately find a job as a writer. Just like the characters in his books, he had to overcome roadblocks and unexpected turns before he finally achieved his dream. The first plot twist sent Yancey to law school. He left after a year to reconsider his options.

Rick Yancey worked summers and weekends as a ranch hand on his family's 200-acre (81 hectares) farm in Central Florida. Yancey said working with cows gave him plenty of time to daydream.

Over the next several years, Yancey held a series of interesting and unusual part-time jobs. Yancey, for example, worked as a typesetter, convenience store manager, and production line worker. His other jobs included English professor, drama teacher, actor, director, playwright, and theater critic.

During the summers, Yancey also worked as a ranch hand for a family business. "It fit in well with being a freelance writer because I had a lot of free time in between gathering up the cows and feeding them to write," Yancey said in an interview with WILL Radio in Illinois.

ADVENTURES WITH THE IRS

When he was twenty-eight, Yancey answered an ad in the Sunday paper for a job with the

Department of the Treasury. Details about the job were sketchy, but it paid nearly three times the amount he had been earning and it only required a college degree. The position turned out to be a revenue officer with what Yancey describes as the most "feared, hated, and maligned agency in the federal government"—the Internal Revenue Service (IRS).

Yancey recalls this experience in his memoir, *Confessions of a Tax Collector: One Man's Tour of Duty Inside the IRS*.

"Why do you want to be a revenue officer?" an IRS officer asked Yancey during his interview in late 1990.

"I need the job," Yancey said.

Rick Yancey worked for the Internal Revenue Service (IRS) for twelve years. He met his wife, Sandy, at the agency. The job also inspired him to write *Confessions of a Tax Collector*.

The IRS officer pointed to the jobs listed on Yancey's résumé. "Playwright. Convenience store manager. Ranch hand," he said. "Anything you haven't done?"

"Singing telegrams," Yancey replied.

The IRS officer wasn't amused. "What do you want to be when you grow up?" he asked.

"I'm a writer," Yancey said. "It's all I ever wanted to be, since I was a little kid."

But the future award-winning author put that dream on hold to become what he called a "cubicle-dwelling, buttoned-down" tax collector for the IRS, according to a story he wrote for the *Gainesville Sun*.

"The little lie I told myself was this IRS gig would be short-lived," Yancey wrote. "I would get serious about my literary ambitions once my feet were planted firmly on the ground of financial security. One year, two tops, and I would finish that blockbuster novel or screenplay and leave a job for which no one could be more ill-suited than me."

Yancey's life, however, took another surprising turn. He stayed at the IRS for twelve years.

LOVE STORY UNFOLDS

Yancey met the hero of his life's story during the second year of his "tour of duty" with the IRS. And his life suddenly added a new, romantic chapter.

Yancey fell in love with an IRS analyst he first saw at a crowded meeting at the federal building in Lakeland, Florida. "I took the one empty seat in the third row, and laid eyes on the most beautiful woman I had ever seen," Yancey wrote in the *Gainesville Sun*.

Three years after that chance meeting, Yancey married the woman he describes as his "light in the darkness"—his wife, Sandy. "Sandy would become the first real champion of my writing," he wrote.

His wife convinced Yancey to take a leap of faith and turn a screenplay he'd written into a novel. When he protested that he wasn't a novelist, his wife refused to listen. "Every excuse, every protest, every denial was met with, 'Oh, just write the book, Rick,'" he recalled.

Five years later, Yancey finally heeded his wife's advice. He opened a spiral notebook and wrote the following words:

A BURNING IN HOMELAND
A novel
By Richard Yancey
(Begun January 20, 2000)

For the next three months, Yancey penned a story in longhand about murder, betrayal, and

ADULT AUTHORS TURNED CHILDREN'S BOOK AUTHORS

Rick Yancey wrote his first two books—*A Burning in Homeland* (2003) and *Confessions of A Tax Collector* (2004)—for adult readers. He also wrote the Highly Effective Detective mystery series, which features a bumbling detective named Teddy Ruzak, for adults. But Yancey isn't the only famous children's book author who started his career writing books for adults. A number of best-selling authors first wrote books for an adult audience before they ventured into the world of children's publishing.

John Grisham is best known for writing legal thrillers such as *The Firm* and *A Time to Kill.* But he's also the author of the Theodore Boone series for young readers.

James Patterson has written more than seventy best-selling crime novels, including the Alex Cross and Women's Murder Club series. In 2007, Patterson started writing books for teens and younger readers. He's since written the highly regarded Maximum Ride, Daniel X, and Witch and Wizard series for teens. He also wrote *I Funny* and other titles in the popular Middle School series.

Dave Barry and Ridley Pearson are the award-winning authors of a popular children's series that began with *Peter and the Starcatchers.* But years before they penned their five-book prequel to Peter Pan, both authors wrote for adults. Barry, for example,

Authors Ridley Pearson *(right)* and Dave Barry *(left)* wrote the popular *Peter and the Starcatchers* series for young readers. Like Rick Yancey, these award-winning authors launched their careers writing for adults.

wrote books such as *You Can't Make This Stuff Up* and the dark comedy *Insane City*. He's also a Pulitzer Prize–winning humor columnist for the *Miami Herald*.

Pearson is a *New York Times* best-selling author of more than twenty-five suspense and crime novels, including *The Pied Piper* and *Cut and Run*. He also writes the children's series Kingdom Keepers about Walt Disney World.

revenge in a small Florida town. When his hand finally gave out, he transcribed the story onto his computer.

Yancey finished his novel a year later. "I was proud, of course," he wrote in the *Gainesville Sun*. "I was also terrified, because the ultimate goal was not the writing of it, but getting it published."

Yancey's wife again gave him the push he needed. She bought him a copy of the guidebook *Getting Your Book Published for Dummies*. "What followed was nearly a year of rejection letters, unreturned phone calls, and unanswered e-mails," Yancey wrote.

The talented author was ready to give up. He was convinced that his writing dream would never come true.

FIRST BOOK PUBLISHED

But in a dramatic turn of events, Yancey received a call from New York literary agent Brian DeFiore. He liked Yancey's writing and wanted to find a publisher for his book.

It didn't take long. In 2003, Simon & Schuster released Yancey's first novel, *A Burning in Homeland*. The book received high praise. *Kirkus Reviews* called it a "Southern gothic…that strikes all the right chords." The magazine also said the novel had shades of such classics as *The Count of Monte Cristo* and *Wuthering Heights*.

But Yancey couldn't afford to quit his job at the IRS and become a full-time author. Not yet, anyway. At this point in his career, Yancey and his wife lived in Knoxville, Tennessee. The IRS transferred the couple there in 1995.

FROM TAX COLLECTOR TO NOVELIST

Yancey continued to spend his days chasing people who hadn't paid their taxes. At night, he wrote about his adventures catching those tax dodgers.

His second book, *Confessions of a Tax Collector*, is based on his twelve-year journey with the IRS. HarperCollins released the memoir in 2004. The book became a best seller and received starred reviews from critics. *The Boston Globe* called *Confessions of a Tax Collector* a "rich mix of humor, horror, and angst that's better than most novels you'll find on the best-seller lists."

Not everyone applauded Yancey's memoir. The IRS frowned on the book. "The IRS doesn't take too kindly to employees talking about their inner workings," Yancey told Knoxville's *Metro Pulse* newspaper.

Yancey left the IRS after the book's release. The time had come to fulfill his dream and become a full-time writer. "I didn't have a trust fund, didn't have the luxury of taking a year or two to write another novel, didn't have a lot of cash to fall back on," Yancey said.

What he did have, though, was his mighty pen that would soon write spellbinding stories about young heroes who battle monsters, aliens, and other forces of evil to save the world.

THE LIFE OF A FULL-TIME WRITER

Today, the celebrated author writes his action-packed adventures,

mysteries, and horror novels from his home in Gainesville, Florida. He and his family moved from

The Hippodrome Theater is a big attraction in Gainesville, Florida, where author Rick Yancey and his family live. Theater is important to Yancey, a former actor, director, playwright, and critic.

Knoxville, Tennessee, to "gator country" in 2005. Yancey and his wife have three sons: Jonathan, Joshua, and Jacob. He says they're the driving forces behind his work and the main source of his literary magic.

Yancey's dogs are another source of magic in his life. They're his constant writing companions and the subject of many of his comments on Facebook and Twitter. Yancey, for example, posted a tribute on Facebook to the family's fourteen-year-old black Lab, Casey, when she died in 2011. "The sweetest dog I have ever known passed away this morning," he wrote. "She was there, literally by my side, for every book. Goodbye, Casey. The squirrels of this world may not grieve your passing, but I will."

A few months later, Yancey found a new best friend and writing dog. He introduced the family's goldendoodle, Max, to his fans on Twitter. "My new writing companion," he wrote. "Max is still in training, but he's got good instincts."

EXTRAORDINARY ADVENTURES

Yancey's own instincts—and ability to craft riveting, fast-paced, suspense-filled stories—sealed his fate as an internationally acclaimed literary star. By May 2013, the multitalented author had written fourteen books. His genres include memoir, mystery, adventure, and horror. Six of his novels are written for adults. But Yancey's most popular books—the ones that etched his name in publishing history and captured the attention of Hollywood—are for younger readers.

Yancey launched his career as one of the most beloved writers for young adults with a high-speed, bloody battle–filled tale. The book is about an unlikely hero named Alfred Kropp and his extraordinary adventures that save the world by accident.

AN UNLIKELY HERO

Rick Yancey didn't set out on a quest to write a book that would rescue young readers from their dull and dreary lives. He never intended to pen a high-octane thriller about an unlucky fifteen-year-old who battles agents of darkness to save the world.

When Yancey sat down to write *The Extraordinary Adventures of Alfred Kropp*, he envisioned an adult novel about a thirty-three-year-old former security guard who becomes a bumbling detective. But the story took on a life of its own, and the clumsy detective led Yancey down a surprising new path.

"Suddenly, in the midst of my writing, with no planning on my part, he finds Excalibur, the sword of King Arthur," Yancey told Bloomsbury Children's Publishing.

Yancey shared this unexpected plot twist with his agent, who came up with an idea that changed the course of the

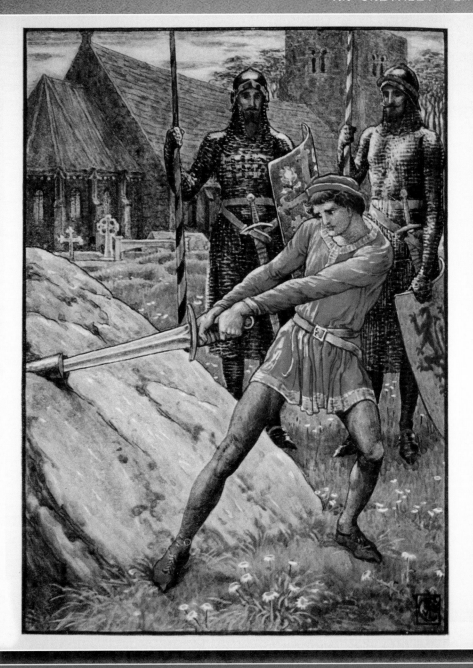

The stories of King Arthur, his legendary blade, Excalibur, and a love of sword-fighting provided the inspiration for Rick Yancey's first young adult novel, *The Extraordinary Adventures of Alfred Kropp.*

author's writing career. He suggested the plot was just right for a young audience.

UNQUALIFIED TO WRITE A YOUNG ADULT NOVEL

But the critically acclaimed author had never written a book for young adults. He was hesitant to journey into those uncharted literary waters. "I'm totally unqualified to write a young adult novel," Yancey told the *Gainesville Sun*. Or so he thought.

Yancey channeled his inner fifteen-year-old boy. He also tapped into his fascination with the legend of King Arthur, the movie *Excalibur*, and sword fighting. "I wanted to write a great adventure story that combined my love for swords with the Arthur stories," Yancey told BookBrowse.com.

Ideas started to unfold: King Arthur, Excalibur. Images started to swirl: sword fights, knights. Yancey soon envisioned an action-packed Arthurian adventure story set in the modern world. He imagined knights driving Ferraris, sword-wielding evildoers dressed in dark, flowing robes, and bloody battles against gun-toting motorcycle madmen.

A HERO IS BORN

Now all Yancey needed was a hero. He didn't want just any hero, though. He wanted the most unlikely hero possible.

Yancey pictured a lumbering, large-headed, down-on-his luck teenager. This fifteen-year-old, shuffled from foster home to foster home after his mother's death, is suddenly plunged into a death-defying mission to return the most powerful sword in history to its rightful place. All of these elements collided to create Yancey's "not very good at anything" hero, Alfred Kropp.

But Yancey first had to overcome his own insecurity and doubts to write Alfred's tale. "I didn't think I could make the voice authentic," he told *Publishers Weekly*.

Yancey used a secret weapon to conquer his writing demons—his three sons. The author relied on feedback he received from his boys, who were twenty, fifteen, and nine when he wrote his debut novel for young adults. Yancey incorporated funny comments his sons made into Alfred's story.

His middle son, Josh, played a pivotal role in the success of Alfred's adventures. According to a 2007 story in the *Gainesville Sun*, Yancey asked Josh—who was the same age as Alfred—to gauge the accuracy of his young hero's voice and actions. In other words, Josh became Yancey's "litmus test" for *The Extraordinary Adventures of Alfred Kropp*.

The story passed with flying colors. Josh couldn't put the book down. His son read Alfred's

THE NAMING OF ALFRED KROPP

Rick Yancey's bumbling hero wasn't always known as Alfred Kropp. Yancey used a different name for the clumsy fifteen-year-old in his original manuscript. He called him Alfred Krupp.

"I wanted [his first name] to sound close to Arthur, but I didn't want it to be Arthur," Yancey said during a presentation to youth at the Orlando Public Library.

The author came up with the name Krupp after reading the word "Krups" on his coffee maker. He toyed with variations of the word and ended up with K-R-U-P-P. "And I said it together and thought it sounded great: Alfred Krupp," Yancey told young fans at the library. "Just saying the name makes you want to laugh or smile."

But Yancey received troubling news about his character's name one month before the book went to press. His publisher learned that Alfred Krupp was a real person who had ties to Nazi Germany. Alfred Krupp owned a company that built tanks, guns, and other weapons for Adolf Hitler during World War II. Hitler was the leader of Nazi Germany, who ordered the execution of six million Jewish people. "We don't think we want to publish a major young adult novel whose protagonist has the same name as a Nazi," Yancey recalled his publisher saying.

The acclaimed author made the "agonizing" decision to change Alfred's name. "It was like changing a child's name," he said.

Yancey wanted to keep his hero's first name as Alfred. His wife, Sandy, came up with Alfred's new last name. She suggested changing the "U" to an "O." Bloomsbury researched the name "Alfred Kropp" and didn't find any ties to Nazis or other worrisome people.

tale in two days. "He promised me it wasn't because I wrote it," Yancey said.

ALFRED KROPP'S EXTRAORDINARY ADVENTURES BEGIN

The Extraordinary Adventures of Alfred Kropp, released in October 2005, struck a similar chord with readers across the county. "With bumbling, lumbering, wisecracking Alfred Kropp by our side, there's never a dull moment on this bumpy ride that proves just how extraordinary 'ordinary' can be," reviewer Joni Rendon wrote on the Web site Teenreads.com.

Publishers Weekly gave Yancey's novel a starred review and called it a standout in the crowded field of fantasy and adventure books. The magazine even compared Yancey and his good-natured protagonist to best-selling author J. K. Rowling and the unlikely hero she created to save the magical world—Harry Potter.

Like the Harry Potter books, *The Extraordinary Adventures of Alfred Kropp* cast an instant spell on readers around the globe. The book immediately sold in twelve countries and was translated into ten languages. (That number has since risen.)

Librarians also praised Yancey's book, which was a finalist for the prestigious Carnegie Medal. The British literary award is given each year to the author of an outstanding book for children.

Alfred Kropp's extraordinary adventures captured the attention of Hollywood, too. Warner Brothers quickly bought the film rights to the book.

Yancey told *Publishers Weekly* that he wanted Alfred's tale to have cinematic appeal. "Ever since I was young, fourteen or fifteen, I wondered if you could write a book that combined the visceral thrill of watching a movie with the total immersion you feel when you're inside a good book," he said.

The movie was originally scheduled to hit box offices in 2007, according to the *Gainesville Sun*. The film was still in development in early 2013.

ATTRACTING READERS

The novel also achieved a lofty goal that Yancey set for the book. It convinced thousand of boys around the world to read. The story's fast cars, loyal knights, and fiery chase scenes lured middle-school age boys away from video games, movies, television, and other activities vying for

Boys around the world started to read instead of play video games after Rick Yancey's thrilling, high-speed book *The Extraordinary Adventures of Alfred Kropp* arrived in bookstores.

their attention. "We need to really start focusing on getting boys back into reading," Yancey told the *Gainesville Sun*.

Although Yancey wrote *The Extraordinary Adventures of Alfred Kropp* for young readers, many adults also became fans of the book and its main character.

One of Alfred's biggest champions was Yancey's editor at Bloomsbury, Julie Romeis. "I fell in love with the character Alfred," she told the *Gainesville Sun*. "I couldn't put [the book] down, and I stayed up until about 3 AM reading it."

THE SEAL OF SOLOMON

Yancey wasn't sure if Alfred's save-the-world saga would become a series when he finished the first adventure. But he was optimistic. "I think there's a lot to be done with Alfred," Yancey told the *Gainesville Sun*.

He was right. Bloomsbury released the second installment of Alfred's journey in May 2007. *Alfred Kropp: The Seal of Solomon* plunges the young hero back into another high-speed, deadly mission. This time, Alfred battles the "nastiest demon to ever roam the earth." He also tracks a rogue secret agent who steals King Solomon's ring, known as the Seal of Solomon, unleashing terrifying evil spirits.

Alfred battles the demons haunting his personal life, too. Those wicked creatures include school bullies—tormentors he had hoped would ignore him after he saved the planet. "I'm just saying I thought my life might be different," the character says in the book. "I was wrong. Of course, nobody knows I had saved the world. I wasn't allowed to tell, and who would believe me if I did?"

The bullies even invent a cruel sport to terrorize Alfred. They call it "Kropping," and it involves everything from tripping him in the hallway to giving him a wedgie.

Bullies aren't the only demons Alfred faces in his private life. Yancey wanted his reluctant hero to tackle the painful, unresolved issues surrounding the death of his mother. She died when Alfred was twelve years old. "I realized after the first book that I had really given short shrift to Alfred's mother's death," Yancey told *Publishers Weekly*. "That would be a really devastating event for a teenage boy."

KING OF CHILDREN'S LITERATURE

Yancey understood that many of his fans—especially the middle-school age boys who devoured his books—might not want to read about Alfred's sensitive side. He knew it was a risk to delve into these emotional issues. But he took a chance—and it paid off. *Alfred Kropp: The Seal of Solomon* continued Yancey's reign as one of the kings of children's literature, especially action-packed thrillers aimed at boys.

Kirkus Reviews hailed Alfred's second adventure. "The world's fastest car, huge CW3XD guns that use bullets laced with Alfred's blood and a death-defying sky dive are only a few of the other action magnets sure to attract middle-school readers," the magazine said.

But Yancey said any praise for the book belonged to his boys. "It was my sons who awakened the slumbering boy in me," he wrote in the book's acknowledgements. "[Each] in his own way leading me down the path that ultimately led to Alfred."

What harrowing adventures awaited Alfred in his next mission to save the world? He'd already found the legendary sword, Excalibur. He'd defeated the evil demon, King Paimon. What dangerous journey would Yancey send Alfred on next?

THE THIRTEENTH SKULL

Fans didn't have to wait long to learn those answers. Bloomsbury released the third

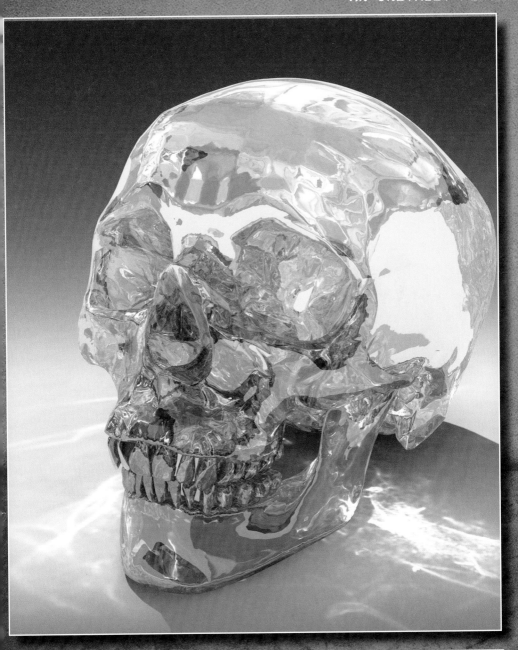

A mystical crystal skull known as the Skull of Doom served as the catalyst for Rick Yancey's *The Thirteenth Skull.* According to legend, there are thirteen crystal skulls. When the ancient artifacts are brought together, they supposedly can unlock the secrets of the universe.

adventure in Yancey's series—*Alfred Kropp: The Thirteenth Skull*—in June 2008. In this ninja-filled saga, Alfred faces a dangerous new enemy and an ancient artifact of doom called the Thirteenth Skull.

Yancey sets the tone for Alfred's bullet-flying journey in the book's opening pages. A delivery truck blows up. Alfred's guardian, Samuel, is shot in the penthouse of Samson Towers. Alfred is injured in a battle with a gun-toting stranger, who later dies in another explosion. Five police officers are killed in a high-speed chase. "And you seem to be the common denominator in all this, Alfred," a police officer tells him after he lands in jail.

The action continues at rapid-fire speed as Alfred risks his life to find Merlin's thirteenth crystal skull, which has the power to destroy the universe. Along his journey, Alfred notices that the people sworn to protect him no longer seem trustworthy. Someone is watching Alfred's every move—and trying to kill him at each turn.

HIGH PRAISE FOR AN UNLIKELY HERO

Young readers and critics cheered *Alfred Kropp: The Thirteenth Skull*. "This book was an amazing

GUYS READ PROJECT

Rick Yancey and his wife are strong supporters of a nationwide program to spark boys' interest in reading. The Web-based literacy project is called Guys Read. "Our mission is to help boys become self-motivated, lifelong readers," its Web site states.

Children's book author Jon Scieszka founded the program, which is designed to introduce boys to books that guys have said they like to read. More information about the project—and lists of books that boys like to read—is available on the Guys Read Web site at http://www.guysread.com.

A volunteer at Sunset Park Elementary School in Wilmington, North Carolina, reads with fourth grader Devin Head, a member of the Guys Read book club designed to encourage boys to read.

read, and I would recommend it to anyone who likes mysteries and humorous fast-paced books," a young reviewer wrote on the *Teen Ink* Web site.

Kirkus Reviews said the thriller was "soaked" with action. "He [Yancey] puts his hero on a galloping horse pursued by roaring motorcycles, dangles him by a cable under a soaring helicopter, and pushes him down a mountain on an inverted garbage-can lid," the magazine said.

It wasn't easy to write all those nail-biting scenes, Yancey told *Publishers Weekly*. He struggled with parts of the book, and sixty pages into the work he turned down what he called a "blind alley."

Yancey also noticed changes in Alfred, who'd become like a fourth son to him. As he wrote the book, Yancey said his teenage hero was sometimes grouchy and temperamental. "I want Alfred to do certain things, and he 'refuses' to do them," he told the *Gainesville Sun*.

What path does Yancey want Alfred to follow in the future? Will he send his oversized hero on more adventures to save the world? "I see the Alfred series as continuing indefinitely," Yancey said in an interview with the Web site 800-CEO-READ.

Yancey stepped away from the world of legendary swords and modern-day knights in 2008 and embarked on a new literary journey. In writing his second acclaimed series, Yancey entered a frightening realm filled with headless, flesh-eating monsters. Keep reading—if you dare. The world you're about to enter is so terrifying that it even gave Yancey nightmares.

THREE

CHASING MONSTERS

The frightening images seemed so real to author Rick Yancey. He can still see the hulking shadow and hear his heart pounding as the faceless beast chases him through his home. These troubling images have haunted the award-winning author since he was a boy, when they appeared to him in a horrifying dream.

"It's odd how the horrible nightmares from childhood stick with us," Yancey said in an interview with MonsterLibrarian.com. "The feeling of being doomed…with the clock ticking down until it caught me…I still remember my terror."

The acclaimed author tapped into those disturbing memories when he ventured into the eerie realm of horror to write his second series for young adults. The four-part saga, which starts with the book *The*

Rick Yancey tapped into the frightening images used in horror movies such as Bram Stoker's *Dracula* to write his chilling *Monstrumologist* series about a boy's haunting journeys with monster slayer Dr. Pellinore Warthrop.

Monstrumologist, takes readers into the dark world of twelve-year-old Will Henry and his chilling journeys with Dr. Pellinore Warthrop, a scientist who hunts monsters and other gruesome creatures of the night.

EERIE VICTORIAN FLAIR

Yancey set his bloodcurdling first volume, *The Monstrumologist*, in a small New England town in the late 1800s. "Once I decided I wanted to write a horror story, immediately my thoughts turned to the nineteenth century," Yancey told MonsterLibrarian.com. "Gas lights and cobblestones, capes and tall hats—it seemed to fit the mood perfectly."

There's another reason Yancey chose this time in history. "The most famous horror novels of all (*Frankenstein* and *Dracula*) were from that period," he said. "Why not journey to the time in which modern horror was born?"

To ensure his books captured the atmosphere of those Victorian days, Yancey immersed himself in the period. He paid close attention to every detail, from the clopping of horse hooves on cobblestone streets to the elegant language used at the turn of the century. He was careful not to include words or elements that did not exist at that time.

The Monstrumologist and its sequels are peppered with words that give the stories a Victorian flair. Those nearly forgotten words include sepulcher (tomb), maw (animal's mouth), effluvia (smell of fumes), leviathan (monster), alienist (psychiatrist), and stygian (pitch black). "More than any book I've written, with each sentence I fought to find the perfect word," Yancey said in an interview with Karen S. Scott of *Carpe Keyboard*.

WRITING BY CANDLELIGHT

But the battle of words didn't last long. The master wordsmith penned the first book in his spine-tingling series—*The Monstrumologist*—in a matter of months. According to the *Gainesville Sun*, Yancey sold the proposal for *The Monstrumologist* to Simon & Schuster Children's Publishing in July 2008. He turned in the final manuscript six months later.

Yancey often worked on his terrifying tale until 3 AM and wrote most of the book by candlelight. Those haunting late-night writing sessions fueled Yancey's imagination. They helped him envision the faceless, flesh-eating anthropophagi that Will Henry and Dr. Warthrop hunt in his gory tale. In the play *Othello*, legendary poet and playwright William Shakespeare describes these cannibals as "men whose heads do grow beneath their shoulders."

WHY SUCH WRETCHED MONSTERS?

Why did Yancey feature such wretched and little-known beasts in his first horror novel for young adults?

"I didn't want Warthrop to be studying or chasing after a 'traditional' cryptid, like a Bigfoot, or anything from supernatural fiction (vampires, werewolves, etc.)," Yancey told MonsterLibrarian.com. "I thought we were up to our literary eyeballs in vampires and the like, and, let's face it, how scary is Bigfoot really?"

Not nearly as scary as the anthropophagi, Yancey said. Writing about the ghastly creatures sent chills down his spine. Grisly images of those monsters dwelling in a dangerous underground labyrinth gave Yancey nightmares. "It gets pretty creepy," he told the *Gainesville Sun*.

The hideous beasts terrify Yancey's young protagonist, who has seen his share of horrifying monsters. "I choked back the bile that rushed from my empty stomach and willed my knees to be still," Will Henry says the first time he sees a dead anthropophagus in Dr. Warthrop's laboratory.

THESE ARE THE SECRETS I HAVE KEPT

The *Monstrumologist* series is told through the eyes of Will Henry, who becomes Dr. Warthrop's apprentice after his parents die in a fire. The monster hunter writes his chilling saga on the pages of thirteen tattered journals. "The journals are composed when he's a much older man looking back at these horrifying events when he was twelve," Yancey told the *Ledger* newspaper.

"A cross between Mary Shelley and Stephen King."
—VOYA

RICK YANCEY

THE MONSTRUMOLOGIST

THERE ARE MONSTERS AMONG US . . .
AND THEY MUST BE FOUND

The Monstrumologist is the first of four books in Rick Yancey's spine-tingling series. The tale describes the horror twelve-year-old Will Henry faces as he helps Dr. Pellinore Warthrop track down the headless, man-eating anthropophagi.

Yancey used the first three journals as the framework for *The Monstrumologist*. "These are the secrets I have kept," Will Henry writes to begin his terrifying tale. "This is the trust I never betrayed."

The journals describe the unimaginable horror that Will Henry and the monstrumologist face in tracking down and destroying the man-eating anthropophagi, which have infested their hometown of New Jerusalem, Massachusetts. Dr. Warthrop summons a dark and evil man named Jack Kearns to help them slay the 7-foot (213 cm), bloodthirsty beasts. But he warns Will Henry that Kearns is a ruthless killer—and not someone whom he could trust. "Steer clear of Dr. John Kearns, Will Henry!" the monstrumologist says. "He is a dangerous man, but the hour calls for dangerous men, and we must use every tool at our disposal."

GOTHIC HORROR AT ITS FINEST

Yancey's terror-filled novel arrived in bookstores nationwide in September 2009. The gory tale attracted a new generation of young readers to the chills of horror novels.

Critics praised *The Monstrumologist* and compared Yancey's book to works by legendary horror writers Mary Shelley, author of *Frankenstein*, and H. P. Lovecraft, the father of modern horror fiction. "This story is gothic horror at its finest and most disturbing," *VOYA* magazine said. "The tale will force readers to stay up late to finish and then remain awake, afraid to shut off the lights."

The American Library Association (ALA) also applauded *The Monstrumologist* and selected it as a Michael L. Printz Honor Book in 2010. The prestigious award recognizes excellence in young adult literature.

The honor caught Yancey by surprise. "I honestly didn't think *The Monstrumologist* was the sort of book that wins prestigious awards," he said in his acceptance speech. "When I was writing it, I would tell my wife how ridiculous it was—"ludicrous" was the word I used."

Self-doubt consumed Yancey as he wrote what he called his "car wreck of a book." "It's bloody, horrific, and disturbing, but you just have to look," Yancey said in his speech. "But to me at least it rises above the miasma of gore, for amid all the blood and guts—and the maggots—is a story of almost inconceivable courage in the face of nearly unimaginable terror."

HUNGER FOR HUMAN FLESH

Yancey continued to fill Will Henry's world with terror in the second book of his spine-chilling series,

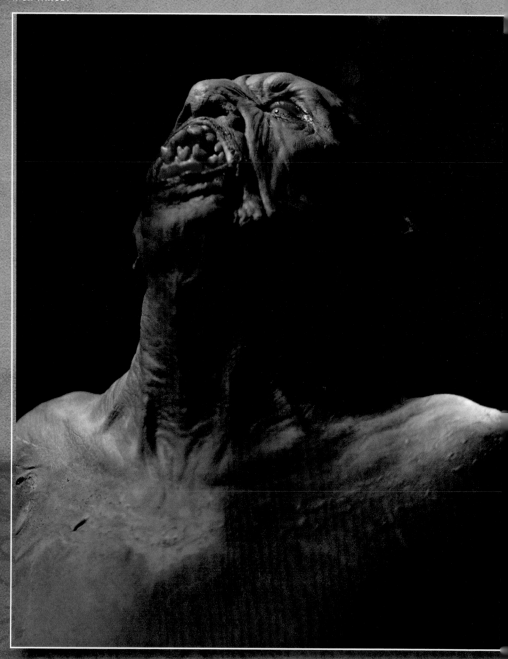

Rick Yancey used the legend of the flesh-eating *Lepto lurconis* as the basis of his terrifying book *The Curse of the Wendigo*. The gruesome wendigo reportedly has an insatiable hunger for human flesh.

The Curse of the Wendigo. In this frightening sequel, Dr. Warthrop and his young apprentice set off in the perilous Canadian wilderness in search of the gruesome, man-eating wendigo—or *Lepto lurconis*.

According to Native American folklore, these vampirelike beasts have a hunger for human flesh that is never satisfied. "(It) starves even as it gorges itself on human flesh," Yancey said in a 2010 interview with the Web site Dread Central.

In the book, Dr. Warthrop calls the wendigo a mystical creature—"no more real than the tooth fairy." But many cultures, he says, tell terrifying tales about these yellow-eyed monsters that eat the skin of their human prey. And many people—including the doctor's Monstrumology Society—argue that these creatures that "devour all mankind" are real.

Can the doctor and Will Henry prove these wicked monsters are nothing more than a myth? Can they find their fellow monstrumologist, who vanishes while searching for these vile beasts? Or will they uncover an even more terrifying truth about the wendigo—and the fate of their missing friend?

AWARD-WINNING THRILLER

Simon & Schuster released *The Curse of the Wendigo* in October 2010. The gothic thriller became an instant hit among teenage horror fans and received rave reviews from critics.

Publishing giant Simon & Schuster published Rick Yancey's acclaimed *Monstrumologist* series.

"The chilling sequel to Yancey's Printz Honor book, *The Monstrumologist*, is as fast-paced, elegant, and, yes, gruesome as its predecessor," *Publishers Weekly* said.

The Curse of the Wendigo captured several awards, including a 2011 selection by the Young Adult Library Services Association (YALSA) as one of the best books for young adults. It was also a finalist in the 2011 *Los Angeles Times* Book Prize for Young Adult Literature.

THE FATHER OF ALL MONSTERS

Yancey took readers on another horror-filled ride in his third book in the *Monstrumologist* series, *The Isle of Blood*. In this terrifying journey, Dr. Warthrop heads to a dangerous island where nests are made from shredded pieces of human flesh and blood rains from the sky. The monstrumologist's quest is set in motion when a terrified man arrives at his door with a mysterious package. Inside that package is the *nidus ex magnificum*—a deadly nest made from human remains.

Anyone who touches the *nidus*—and is exposed to the "rot of stars" used to preserve it—faces an agonizing death. Flesh rots off their bones. Pus oozes from their bodies. And they turn into "cannibalistic zombies."

In the world of monstrumology, the *nidus ex magnificum* is one of the greatest finds. But there's an even bigger prize for scientists who hunt monsters. It's the *Typhoeus magnificum*, the horrible beast that creates the *nidus*.

The famed Dr. Warthrop is determined to find and capture this "father of all monsters." He doesn't take Will Henry with him on his perilous journey, though. He leaves his young apprentice in New York. A new assistant named Thomas Arkwright joins the doctor on his dangerous quest for the "Faceless One of a Thousand Faces."

IN SEARCH OF THE MONSTRUMOLOGIST

Months later, Arkwright returns with news that Dr. Warthrop is dead. Will Henry isn't convinced. He

Actor Steven Boyer narrated the audio versions of the books in the *Monstrumologist* series. The audiobooks made the American Library Association's list of Amazing Audiobooks for Young Adults.

doesn't trust Arkwright and sets out on his own mission to find the doctor.

Will Henry's journey leads him to one of the most frightening and mysterious places on earth—the Isle of Blood. It's an island plagued with infections that could destroy the human race. It's also the place where Will Henry confronts the "most terrible monster of all." Can Will Henry overcome his darkest fears and save the doctor—and himself—from a fate worse than death?

Yancey's monstrous tale again cast a haunting spell on readers and left them hungry for more. *VOYA* magazine hailed *The Isle of Blood* as "an excellent addition to an amazing series."

Kirkus gave the horror novel a starred review. "Articulately literary, horrifically grotesque, and mind-bendingly complex," the magazine said.

Kirkus selected *The Isle of Blood* as one of the Best Teen Books of 2011. *School Library Journal* picked Yancey's horror novel as a Favorite Book Read in 2011. *The Isle of Blood* also made YALSA's list of Amazing Audiobooks for Young Adults in 2013. Actor Steven Boyer narrated the frightening novel.

SECRETS REVEALED

Yancey, however, wasn't finished scaring readers out of their minds. Simon & Schuster released the fourth tale in the *Monstrumologist* series—*The Final Descent*—in September 2013. Yancey structured the thriller as the last three journals that Will Henry writes about his frightening journeys with the monstrumologist. The young monster hunter had already battled flesh-eating, faceless, zombie-making beasts. What other horrors awaited Will Henry and the doctor?

Yancey was almost too afraid to find out. "My heart began to race, and I was suddenly overwhelmed with a desire to simply turn away…to not finish the three remaining journals," Yancey wrote in the epilogue to *The Isle of Blood*.

But Yancey didn't turn away. He couldn't. Will Henry's tale held him captive in an icy grip. Yancey had to find out what happened to the young apprentice in his final, horror-filled journey with the monstrumologist.

What Yancey discovered chilled him to the bone. "I reach now for the end," Will Henry writes in his last journal. "[But] the end will not reach now for me." Those haunting words provide the first clues that something terrible is happening to Will Henry.

"Warthrop sees it, and even Warthrop is afraid," Yancey said in an interview with the blog *Bookshelves of Doom*. "The fourth book explores

FANS SAVE THE MONSTRUMOLOGIST SERIES

The award-winning *Monstrumologist* series almost came to an abrupt end before author Rick Yancey finished his terror-filled tale. Yancey originally signed a three-book contract with Simon & Schuster to write the horror series about young Will Henry and his frightening adventures with monstrumologist Pellinore Warthrop.

As he wrote the series, Yancey discovered he needed one more book to finish his chilling saga. But shortly before Simon & Schuster released the third novel in the series—*The Isle of Blood*—the company refused to make a deal with him for a fourth *Monstrumologist* book.

The decision surprised Yancey. "I clearly say in the epilogue [of book three] that there are more notebooks of Will Henry's—there's more to the story," he said in an August 2011 interview with the *Bookshelves of Doom* blog.

According to Yancey, Simon & Schuster cited low sales and told his agent it had already "spent too much money on the books."

The move ignited a firestorm among Yancey's fans. Book blogger Stephanie Oakes urged readers to contact Simon & Schuster and voice their concerns. "For such an innovative series to be cut short, when the author has said he's champing at the bit to write more is devastating as a reader, a writer, and member of the YA [young adult] community," Oakes wrote.

Other fans and members of the YA community jumped on the "Save the Monstrumologist" bandwagon. The campaign worked. Simon & Schuster changed its mind in a matter of days. "In case you haven't heard, publisher hears voices of fans, decides to publish 4th volume of the Monstrumologist," Yancey tweeted on August 19, 2011. "All credit to the fans."

Simon & Schuster released *The Final Descent*—the last installment in the *Monstrumologist* series—in September 2013.

this—and, of course, will answer the riddle of the notebooks and who Will Henry really is. I think readers will be shocked."

Yancey slayed more monsters—and spooked even more readers—in his third series for young adults. The monsters in these books, however, weren't from this planet. Yancey's next wave of writing took him into the chilling realm of science fiction.

FOUR

CHAPTER

THE NEXT WAVE OF WRITING

What is your greatest fear? That's the question author Rick Yancey asked his wife one evening. It's an interesting question coming from a writer who'd sent chills down the spines of millions of young readers with his haunting tales of blood-thirsty, flesh-eating monsters.

But Yancey's wife didn't list hideous, headless beasts as the source of her greatest fear. Sandy Yancey told her husband that something else—something not of this world—frightened her more than gruesome anthropophagi or demonic wendigos.

"She said an alien abduction," Yancey told *Publishers Weekly*. "She thought that not only would it be terrifying to be abducted, but she'd be afraid no one would believe her!"

His wife's answer triggered a flood of story ideas and a new wave of writing for

64

the best-selling author. What if aliens invaded the planet, Yancey wondered. What if cold, calculating creatures from another world abducted your friends, neighbors, and even your family members? What would happen to them? Would you ever see them again?

Yancey's mind raced. Images of a terrified girl running through the barren countryside came into focus. Who was she? What was she running from? And why was she so scared?

Yancey's thoughts returned to the possibility of an alien invasion. How would extraterrestrials attack the planet? Would it happen all at once—or in stages? And was that frightened girl one of the last survivors?

THE 5TH WAVE IS COMING

Those chilling images served as the inspiration for Yancey's third acclaimed series for young adults. Putnam Books for Young Readers released the first book in his sci-fi trilogy—The 5th Wave—in May 2013. This mystery thriller introduces readers to a tough, teenage girl named Cassie Sullivan. She is one of the few people who survive after aliens invade the planet. The cruel creatures attack Earth in different waves—each one more deadly than the previous assaults. During the fourth wave of attack, for example, the aliens

Rick Yancey ventured into the shadowy realm of science fiction in his book *The 5th Wave*. The sci-fi thriller follows a teenage girl who manages to survive after aliens invade Earth.

unleash an army of murderous creatures that look like humans. These Silencers roam the planet in search of survivors and kill anyone they see.

For Cassie Sullivan, the world becomes a dark, desolate, and dangerous planet. Her parents are dead and her younger brother is missing. She learns the only way to stay alive is to trust no one. Anyone could be a deadly Silencer—even the mysterious Evan Walker, who offers to help Cassie rescue her brother. Can she trust this charming stranger? Is he the only hope she has to save her brother—and herself?

FIRST JOURNEY INTO THE REALM OF SCIENCE FICTION

The 5th Wave marked Yancey's first writing journey into the world of science fiction. But the master storyteller grew up reading books by sci-fi "giants" such as Robert Heinlein (*Stranger in a Strange Land*) and Arthur C. Clarke (*2001: A Space Odyssey*).

"Science fiction is one of my first loves, along with fantasy," Yancey told *Publishers Weekly* in a November 2012 interview.

Yancey, however, didn't want to rehash any of the genre's worn-out tales about extraterrestrials that attack the planet. He wanted to put his own spin on the "aliens invade Earth" story line. "For this novel, I wanted to think through what a plausible alien invasion might look like, versus a Hollywood version," he told *Publishers Weekly*.

Yancey achieved that goal—and much more. After reading just a few pages of *The 5th Wave*, Jennifer Besser, vice president and publisher of Putnam Books for Young Readers, knew she had a best seller in her hands.

THE NEXT BIG PHENOMENON

Putnam moved quickly to buy Yancey's alien invasion masterpiece. In March 2012, the publishing

Arthur C. Clarke, who penned the classic *2001: A Space Odyssey*, is considered one of the greatest science-fiction writers of the twentieth century. Rick Yancey grew up reading Clarke's books.

powerhouse reportedly paid seven figures for the haunting three-book series, according to *Publishers Weekly*. "*The 5th Wave* is a publisher's dream," Besser told the magazine.

Putnam launched a massive public relations campaign to promote Yancey's trilogy, which has UFO lore woven throughout the pages. During the first wave of its media blitz, the company released early copies of Yancey's novel to editors in the United States and around the world. Putnam sold the epic sci-fi thriller to publishers in at least seventeen countries, including Germany, France, Italy, and Israel.

The 5th Wave became a top pick among international editors at the October 2012 Frankfurt Book Fair. The legendary fair, held in Germany, is the world's largest marketplace for books. Editor Lippo Luukkonen from Finland predicted *The 5th Wave* would be the "next big phenomenon on the YA market."

THE 5TH WAVE INVADES THE UNITED STATES

Yancey's suspense-filled novel received similar waves of support in the United States—months before its May 2013 invasion of bookstores nationwide. The January 2013 issue of *Publishers Weekly* named *The 5th Wave* one of the "most anticipated books" of the year. Shanta Newlin, director of publicity for Penguin Young Readers group, said science fiction novels like *The 5th Wave* would be the "next big thing" in children's literature.

In the final waves of publicity for *The 5th Wave*, Putnam released nationwide ads about the gripping novel in newspapers, theaters, and on television. The company announced it would print five hundred thousand copies of the highly anticipated book in its initial run.

Throughout that media frenzy, Yancey dropped hints about the book to fans on Facebook. In October 2012, Yancey posted an image on Facebook that read: "The 1st Wave: Lights Out. The Second Wave: Surf's Up. The Third Wave: Pestilence. The Fourth Wave: Silencers. The 5th Wave: Is Coming." Next to the picture, Yancey wrote: "Okay, folks, this is NOT, I repeat, NOT the cover, but a little teaser for my Next Big Thing."

Yancey also discussed his terrifying tale on Twitter. In January 2013, the acclaimed author posted a tweet about his wife's reaction to his chilling novel. "My wife tells me The #5thwave gave her nightmares," he wrote. "Don't know whether to take that as a criticism or a compliment."

DID YOU KNOW?

Here are some lesser-known facts about author Rick Yancey:

- He's an award-winning screenwriter. Yancey wrote a screenplay in the early 1990s that won a prize at the Austin Film Festival. He was a finalist for a Nicholl Fellowship, which is awarded to screenwriters by the Academy of Motion Picture Arts and

Elijah Wood plays Frodo Baggins in the film *The Lord of the Rings: The Fellowship of the Ring*. Frodo Baggins is Rick Yancey's favorite hero in fiction.

Sciences. He's also writing the screenplay for the movie based on *The 5th Wave*, according to the Web site ComingSoon.com.

- He has a sweet tooth. His favorite foods include sherbet, fudge pop tarts, and Oreo cookies.
- His favorite subject in school was reading, and his least favorite subject was math.
- His favorite authors for young adults are: Libba Bray (*The Diviners*), Louis Sachar (*Holes*), and Markus Zusak (*The Book Thief*).
- His favorite hero in fiction is Frodo Baggins from J. R. R. Tolkien's *The Lord of the Rings*.
- He doesn't have a favorite character in his books. "That's like asking which kid I like the best," Yancey said. "I like them all in different ways."
- His motto is: "Never give up."
- He likes to hear from fans and encourages them to contact him on his Web site, http://www .rickyancey.com, or on his Facebook fan page.

Waves of support for Yancey's sci-fi saga rippled through Hollywood, too. GK Films bought the movies rights to the alien invasion trilogy in March 2012, shortly after Yancey inked his seven-figure deal with Putnam. A release date for the film, however, had not been announced as of early 2013.

Hollywood also planned to make a movie based on Yancey's sci-fi short story, "When First We Were Gods," according to a story on the Deadline

Hollywood Web site. The story is about a future society that unlocks the keys to immortality. But only the wealthy are allowed to undergo the process that makes individuals live forever.

WRITING SECRETS

Throughout his career, Yancey has struck a powerful chord with young readers. He's made them believe in the most unlikely heroes. He's introduced them to unimaginable terror. He's even made some readers look up warily at the night sky and wonder if they're really alone in the universe.

But what's Yancey's secret? What's the source of his writing power? And how can other aspiring authors tap into that magic?

The first step is to destroy the "monster" that haunts many writers, Yancey said during a 2007 presentation at the Orlando Public Library. He called this hideous beast the demon of self-doubt. "[It's] the little voice that says you're not good enough, smart enough, talented enough, lucky enough," Yancey told the young audience.

Many writers need to slay another monster that interferes with their success, Yancey continued. This creature is called procrastination. But there's an easy way to defeat that monster, Yancey explained. Write something every day.

Yancey graphically described the anxiety he faces when he doesn't follow that advice. "I have this restless, gnawing fear that I might be sucked into a rogue black hole and never be able to write again," he said in a 2012 interview with E. F. Jace of the blog *Verbose Veracity*.

WRITING HABITS

One of Yancey's favorite places to write is on the patio by his pool. When his three sons were younger, he often wrote on his laptop during their soccer practices, karate lessons, or while he waited to pick them up from school.

Yancey said there were periods when he wrote only at night. He penned much of *The Monstrumologist* late into the evening and early morning hours. "And let me tell you, at three in the morning, monsters are real," Yancey said in an interview with the blog *A Good Addiction*.

In recent years, however, Yancey said he writes "whenever and wherever" he can. He pens first drafts in the morning and then he rereads and edits his novels at night.

Yancey told *Publishers Weekly* that he rarely outlines his books. He said outlines bore him and make him feel like he's "wearing a straightjacket." Yancey doesn't write profiles of his characters either. He wants his characters to reveal themselves naturally—through action and dialogue. "One of the best feelings you get as a writer is when your character does something totally unexpected," Yancey told *Verbose Veracity*.

The award-winning author uses another technique when he writes scenes that are tough to visualize. He acts out those scenes—and often embarrasses his sons in the process. Yancey, for example, grabbed his son's toy sword and acted out a climactic sword-fighting scene in *The Extraordinary Adventures of Alfred Kropp*. He played Alfred and the "bad guy," Mogart, in the scene.

Yancey, however, was too "squeamish" to act out the terrifying scenes in *The Monstrumologist* novel. "The book would have ended up as one long 'AAAAHHHHH!'" he told the MonsterLibrarian.com.

Music also plays a role in Yancey's writing life—and its success. He listens to music or hums his own tunes while he works. He played the soundtrack from the movie *Speed* while he acted out the pivotal sword-fighting scene in his first Alfred Kropp novel.

Rick Yancey attended the 2013 Book Expo America to promote his first science-fiction novel for young adults, *The 5th Wave*. The alien-inspired thriller became an instant best seller.

THE JOY AND PAIN OF WRITING

Although Yancey is a master storyteller and the words in his novels seem to flow effortlessly, he said the process of writing a book is never easy. "Everything is difficult," he told *Verbose Veracity*. "Sometimes the beginning more so than the end; sometimes it's the other way around." Yancey often posts comments on Twitter about his writing struggles. "40 minutes on a single sentence," he tweeted in December 2012.

Yancey, however, said there are good days when a story seems to write itself. Those are his favorite days as a writer. "One of the joys of a really good book is that you're so into the world of the book, you forget what you're looking at is words on a page," Yancey told *Publishers Weekly*.

The best way for writers to find that magic, Yancey said, is to write stories they'd enjoy reading. Forget the latest fads and trends. Write *your* story. "I just write the stories I want to read but nobody has written," he told MonsterLibrarian.com.

In an interview with Goodreads.com, Yancey offered aspiring writers one final piece of advice: "Expect to fail; write as if you've already succeeded." Yancey has done both in his career. He

battled rejection and failure early in his writing journey. But he never gave up. Yancey kept writing the
kinds of stories he would have wanted to read when
he was younger. And those stories changed the face
of young adult literature. They made it more fun.
They made it more terrifying. And they took it places
that have rarely been explored.

Today, Rick Yancey is one of the most popular
children's book authors in the country. Not bad for
a person who told Dread Central, "I'm just a normal
guy with a fascination for abnormal things."

ON RICK YANCEY

Legal name: John Richard Yancey

Birth date: November 4, 1962

Birthplace: Miami, Florida

Current residence: Gainesville, Florida

Marital status: Married to Sandy Yancey

Children: Jonathan, Joshua, and Jacob

Parents: Quillian and Norma Yancey (deceased)

Siblings: Jay Yancey (brother), Lynn Suzanne Burry (sister)

Education: Graduated from Roosevelt University in Chicago with a degree in English

First publication: *A Burning in Homeland*, published in 2003 by Simon & Schuster.

Hobbies: Reading, traveling, hanging out with his family, and working on puzzles. Yancey reads more nonfiction than fiction. He enjoys biographies and books about history, science, and politics.

Interesting facts: Yancey's favorite horror movies are *The Exorcist* and *Silence of the Lambs*. He had trouble sleeping after watching the movie *Paranormal Activity*. Yancey didn't use his real name when he worked as a tax collector for the Internal Revenue Service. He used a name approved by the federal government. It usually takes Yancey six to nine months to write a novel. But it took him a little more than a year to write *The Extraordinary Adventures of Alfred Kropp*. If he could have one superpower, he'd like to be able to fly.

Funniest comment from a fan: "I bought your book from a book fair for $5. Thank you for writing such a cheap book."

Biggest sale: Yancey reportedly sold his *5th Wave* sci-fi trilogy for seven figures.

ON RICK YANCEY'S WORK

The Extraordinary Adventures of Alfred Kropp. New York, NY: Bloomsbury, 2005.

Released: September 15, 2005

Summary: Bumbling teenager Alfred Kropp becomes the most unlikely of heroes after he is roped into stealing King Arthur's legendary sword, Excalibur. When Alfred unknowingly hands the sword over to a man with evil plans, the fifteen-year-old embarks on a dangerous and extraordinary journey to return Excalibur to its rightful place. In this high-speed adventure, Alfred battles modern-day, sword-wielding knights, gun-toting thugs on motorcycles, and evil agents of darkness in a death-defying mission to save the world.

Sales: Bloomsbury originally sold *The Extraordinary Adventures of Alfred Kropp* in twelve countries and translated the book into ten languages. The novel is now translated into at least seventeen languages.

Movie deal: Warner Brothers bought the movie rights to the book. The movie had not been released as of early 2013.

Awards and honors: *Publishers Weekly* Best Books of 2005, *Publishers Weekly* Listen-Up Awards (2006), Texas Lone Star Reading List Selection, Sunshine State Reading List Selection, BookSense Pick, Finalist for the Carnegie Medal

Alfred Kropp: The Seal of Solomon. New York, NY: Bloomsbury, 2007.

Released: June 4, 2007

Summary: Alfred Kropp returns for another high-speed, death-defying adventure. This time, the oversized hero is in pursuit of a rogue agent who has stolen two deadly ancient artifacts: King Solomon's ring and a sacred vessel that has imprisoned the fallen angels of heaven for thousands of years. When Alfred allows the ring to fall into the wrong hands, the world faces imminent danger. The fifteen-year-old underachiever risks his life to get the ring back. But can he defeat a terrible demon known as King Paimon? Can this reluctant hero save the world again?

Alfred Kropp: The Thirteenth Skull. New York, NY: Bloomsbury, 2008.

Released: September 1, 2008

le

es aorebc

Summary: Danger never ends for lumbering teenage hero Alfred Kropp, who is back for a third deadly adventure. The action-packed tale kicks into high gear in the opening pages when an assassin kills Alfred's legal guardian, a former top agent with the secretive Office of Interdimensional Paradoxes and Extraordinary Phenomena (OIPEP). But that's only part of Alfred's problems. He discovers someone is trying to kill him. And the people sworn to protect Alfred no longer seem trustworthy. The action intensifies as Alfred risks his life to find Merlin's thirteenth crystal skull, which has the power to destroy the universe. The fate of the world again rests in the hands of this unlikely teenage hero.

The Monstrumologist. New York, NY: Simon & Schuster Books for Young Readers, 2009.

Released: September 22, 2009

Summary: In 1888, a twelve-year-old orphan named Will Henry becomes an apprentice to a scientist who studies and hunts monsters. In this first chilling adventure, Will Henry and monstrumologist Pellinore Warthrop face unimaginable horror and danger as they journey into the darkness of an underground labyrinth to battle the flesh-eating, headless anthropophagi.

Possible movie deal: Hollywood expressed an interest in making a movie based on *The Monstrumologist*.

By early 2013, however, the movie had not been released.

Awards and honors: Michael L. Printz Honor Book (2010), ALA Best Books for Young Adults (2010), ALA's Amazing Audiobooks for Young Adults (2010), Michigan Library Association Thumbs Up! Honor Book (2010), Amelia Elizabeth Walden Award Nominee (2010)

The Curse of the Wendigo. New York, NY: Simon & Schuster Books for Young Readers, 2010.

Released: October 19, 2010

First printing: One hundred thousand copies

Summary: Will Henry and the Dr. Pellinore Warthrop head to the desolate Canadian wilderness to rescue a fellow monstrumologist who disappears while searching for a gruesome, man-eating creature called the wendigo. According to Native American lore, these monsters have an appetite for human flesh that is never satisfied. Dr. Warthrop doesn't believe the wendigos are real. But he and Will Henry discover a horrifying truth about the wendigo—and the fate of their missing colleague—during their perilous journey.

Awards and honors: ALA's Best Fiction for Young Adults (2011), ALA's Amazing Audiobooks for Young

Adults (2012), *Booklist* Editors' Choice: Books for
Youth (2010), Finalist for the Los Angeles Times Book
Prize for Young Adult Literature (2011), *Kirkus* Star

The Isle of Blood. New York, NY: Simon & Schuster
Books for Young Readers, 2011.
Released: September 13, 2011
Summary: Dr. Pellinore Warthrop embarks on a
terrifying journey to find the "holy grail" of monstrumology—a creature that makes a deadly nest out
of human flesh. But the doctor leaves his young
apprentice, Will Henry, in New York. He takes a new
apprentice named Thomas Arkwright on this dangerous quest. When Arkwright returns with news
that the doctor has died, Will Henry doesn't believe
him. He sets out on a mission to find the doctor.
Will Henry's journey takes him to the frightening
Isle of Blood, which is plagued with infections that
could destroy mankind. The island is also where Will
Henry must battle the "most terrible monster of all."
But can Will Henry save himself—and the doctor—
from a fate worse than death?
Awards and honors: YALSA's Readers' Choice List
(2012), ALA's Top Ten Amazing Audiobooks for
Young Adults (2013), *Kirkus* Star

The Final Descent. New York, NY: Simon & Schuster
Books for Young Readers, 2013.

Released: September 10, 2013

Summary: In this last installment of Yancey's *Monstrumologist* series, Dr. Pellinore Warthrop makes a chilling discovery: something terrible is happening to his young apprentice, Will Henry. It's something so frightening that even the famous monstrumologist is scared. The final tale reveals all the secrets that Will Henry recorded in his journals about his terrifying journeys with the montrumologist and their battles against hideous, headless, man-eating creatures.

The 5th Wave. New York, NY: G.P. Putnam's Sons, 2013.

Released: May 7, 2013

First printing: Five hundred thousand copies

Summary: Rick Yancey enters the realm of science fiction for the first time in this chilling story about a fifteen-year-old girl who survives after aliens invade Earth. At the dawn of the fifth wave of attacks, Cassie Sullivan is on the run from "the Others," aliens who look like humans and kill everyone they see. Cassie has learned the only way to survive is to trust no one. But that changes when she meets a mysterious boy who offers to help rescue her younger brother. Can Cassie trust this boy? Or is he a deadly alien who wants to kill her, too? This is the first installment in Yancey's sci-fi series, which has a romantic twist to the story line.

Movie deal: GK Films bought the movie rights to *The 5th Wave* in March 2012.

Awards and honors: Named one of the "most anticipated books of 2013" by *Publishers Weekly*.

CRITICAL REVIEWS

The Extraordinary Adventures of Alfred Kropp (2005)

"Inventive and delightfully original, this fast-paced tale plants ancient legend in a modern world filled with speeding Ferraris and knights in business suits."—*The Seattle Post-Intelligencer*, November 21, 2005

"Yancey has hit one out of the park with this original, engaging, and sequel-worthy read."—*Kirkus Reviews*, October 1, 2005

"This story of a 'big-headed loser' is as funny as it is scary. Alfred's adventures are not the only element of this tale that is extraordinary—the reluctant hero is, too."—*Publishers Weekly*, August 29, 2005

"A white-knuckle, page-turning read."—*Booklist*, August 2005

Alfred Kropp: The Seal of Solomon (2007)

"A great book for boys, as well as reluctant readers, *The Seal of Solomon* tells a rip-roaring story that teens will love and won't be able to put down."—*School Library Journal*, June 1, 2007

"The emotional core of this novel involves likeable Alfred's unresolved issues about the death of his mother at age twelve, and his sense of loss is palpably heartbreaking. The villain Arnold's issues remain far murkier, his motivation subsumed by the same Hollywood action-flick pyrotechnics—explosive showdowns, multiple near-brushes with death—that made the first book a hit with kids who might otherwise be playing video games."—*Publishers Weekly*, April 2, 2007

"Alfred's unflappably droll humor combines with nonstop, high-powered action as he faces his greatest fears, refuses to be seduced by his fondest dreams, and finds the courage, strength, and willpower to 'look . . . away from the demon's eyes.'"—*VOYA*, June 2007

Alfred Kropp: The Thirteenth Skull (2008)

"Fast-paced from start to finish, with numerous chase scenes (by car, horse, and other means), flying bullets, betrayals, and more, this is a great book for action fans and reluctant readers."—*School Library Journal*, November 2008

"With nonstop action, wry humor, and enough plot 'zigs' instead of 'zags,' this rollicking page-turner is just plain fun."—*VOYA*, June 2008

The Monstrumologist (2009)

"Yancey's elegant depiction of an America plagued with monsters, human and otherwise, spares no grisly detail...Horror lovers will be rapt."—*Publishers Weekly*, September 7, 2009

"This story is gothic horror at its finest and most disturbing. A cross between Mary Shelley and Stephen King, the tale will force readers to stay up late to finish and then remain awake, afraid to shut off the lights."–*VOYA*, February 2010

"Yancey takes the gore and violence of Darren Shan's *Cirque du Freak* (Little, Brown) or Joseph Delaney's Last Apprentice series (HarperCollins) to thrilling new levels in this sophisticated tale." —*School Library Journal*, November 2009

"With numerous nods to H. P. Lovecraft and other literary and historic figures, Will's intelligent diary captures their page-turning, nightmarish adventures." —*Kirkus Reviews*, September 2009

"With a roaring sense of adventure and enough viscera to gag the hardiest of gore hounds, Yancey's series starter might just be the best horror novel of the year." —*Booklist*, September 2009

The Curse of the Wendigo (2010)

"Yancey maintains his excellent, literary fiction style in this horrifying story of a new monster...whose appetite for human flesh is only heightened each time he consumes a new victim." —*VOYA*, December 2010

"As in *The Monstrumologist*, the descriptions of the monster's work are not for the squeamish, offering hours of delightful fun for historical horror fans."—*Library Journal*, October 21, 2010

"The Printz Honor winner slam dunks the blend of horror with science and legend, creating a horrifically believable tale…a page-turner of a historical horror that will simultaneously thrill readers and make them sick to their stomachs."—*Kirkus Reviews*, September 2010

The Isle of Blood (2011)

"This is an excellent addition to an amazing series. The language is perfect, era-appropriate, and wryly humorous. The details are gruesome and horrific and not for the squeamish. The action is exciting and well-paced. The characters, their relationships, and the moral dilemmas they face, however, are the true hub of the story…This is a wonderful book, and readers will yearn for the next in the series."—*VOYA*, December 2011

"The relationship between Will and his master has never been more complex…Yancey's skill as a stylist cannot be denied."—*Booklist*, August 2011

"A wonderful mix of period fiction and gothic horror."—*The Horn Book*, November 1, 2011

"An especially good example of the wit, social criticism, and character development that has elevated this to a prizewinning series; though, like Will, we know something unspeakable always lurks just behind the first shadow in the drawing room." —*The Barnes & Noble Review*, October 28, 2011

The 5th Wave (2013)

"Yancey's heartfelt, violent, paranoid epic, filled with big heroics and bigger surprises, is part *War of the Worlds*, part *Starship Troopers*, part *Invasion of the Body Snatchers*, and part *The Stand*...a sure thing for reviewers and readers alike." —*Booklist*, February 1, 2013

"The plot flips back and forth with so much action and so many expert twists that readers will constantly question whom they can trust and whom they can't. Best of all, everything feels totally real, and that makes it all the more riveting. Nothing short of amazing." —*Kirkus Reviews*, April 1, 2013

"Rick Yancey's *The 5th Wave* is a remarkable, not-to-be-missed-under-any-circumstances book in part because it manages to describe an invasion by aliens—or in 5th Wave-speak, 'the Others'—and leave you thinking, 'Oh, so this is how things will actually happen.'" —*Entertainment Weekly*, May 1, 2013

1962 Rick Yancey is born on November 4 in Miami, Florida. He grows up in Lakeland, Florida.

1976 Yancey pens a twenty-five-page story about a man lost in the swamp and decides he wants to become a writer. He writes the story for his junior high language arts class.

1980 Yancey graduates from Lakeland High School in Lakeland, Florida.

1987 Yancey graduates from Roosevelt University with a degree in English. (He said in *Confessions of a Tax Collector* that he earned his four-year degree in seven years.)

1990 Yancey interviews for a job with the Internal Revenue Service (IRS) in November.

1991 Yancey starts work in January as a tax collector for the IRS.

1993 Yancey meets his future wife, Sandy. She also works for the IRS.

1995 The IRS transfers Yancey and his family to Knoxville, Tennessee.

1996 Yancey starts work on *A Burning in Homeland*.

2003 Simon & Schuster releases *A Burning in Homeland*.

2004 HarperCollins releases *Confessions of a Tax Collector*. Yancey leaves his job at the IRS.

2005 Yancey and his family move to Gainesville, Florida. Bloomsbury U.S.A. Children's Books releases *The Extraordinary Adventures of Alfred Kropp*.

2007 Bloomsbury U.S.A. Children's Books releases *The Seal of Solomon.*

2008 Bloomsbury U.S.A. Children's Books releases *The Thirteenth Skull.*

2009 Simon & Schuster Books for Young Readers releases *The Monstrumologist.*

2010 Simon & Schuster Books for Young Readers releases *The Curse of the Wendigo.*

2011 Simon & Schuster Books for Young Readers releases *The Isle of Blood.*

2012 Putnam buys the rights to Yancey's sci-fi trilogy in a reported seven-figure deal. *The 5th Wave* is the first book in that series. GK Films also buys the movie rights to *The 5th Wave.*

2013 Putnam releases *The 5th Wave* in May. Simon & Schuster releases *The Final Descent*—the fourth and final book in the *Monstrumologist* series—in September.

GLOSSARY

ANGST Anxiety; dread.

ANTHROPOPHAGI Eaters of human flesh; cannibals.

ARTHURIAN Relating to King Arthur and his Knights of the Round Table.

BLOCKBUSTER A book, play, or film that is a huge success.

BUMBLE To stumble or proceed unsteadily.

CLIMACTIC Relating to a climax; exciting or decisive.

CRYPTID A creature or plant whose existence has been suggested but is not yet recognized by science.

DEMON An evil spirit; a tormenting force or passion.

DESOLATE A place that is bare or deserted.

EPILOGUE A short section at the end of a book.

EXTRATERRESTRIAL A living being from somewhere other than Earth.

FORESHADOW To indicate or suggest something before it happens.

GORE Gruesomeness depicted in vivid detail.

HARROWING Causing feelings of fear, horror, or distress.

IMMORTALITY Eternal life or existence.

LITMUS TEST An important indication of future success or failure.

LUMBER To walk or move in a heavy, clumsy manner.

MONSTRUMOLOGY A term used by Rick Yancey to refer to the study of life-forms generally malevolent to humans and not recognized by science as actual organisms, specifically those considered products of myth and folklore; the act of hunting such creatures.

NIDUS A nest in which spiders or insects deposit eggs; a site in the body at which an infection develops.

PIVOTAL Vitally important.

PLAUSIBLE Having an appearance of truth; believable.

PREQUEL A book about an earlier part of a story or a character's life.

PRESTIGIOUS Important, honored, or esteemed.

PROTAGONIST The main character in a story.

QUEST A journey in search of something.

RELUCTANT Showing hesitation or unwillingness to do something.

ROGUE A dishonest or dangerous person; scoundrel.

SEQUEL A book that continues the story established in a previous book.

SHARECROPPER A tenant farmer who gives a share of the crops grown to the landowner instead of rent.

SWASHBUCKLING Full of adventure and excitement.

TRIBUTE Something said or given to show gratitude, praise, or admiration.

TYPESETTER Someone who sets type for printing; a printer.

UNSAVORY Immoral; distasteful.

VILE Disgusting; wicked.

VISCERAL Instinctive or emotional.

Horror Writers Association (HWA)
244 5th Avenue, Suite 2767
New York, NY 10001
Web site: http://www.horror.org/index.php
The Horror Writers Association is a nonprofit organization of writers and publishing professionals around
the world who are dedicated to promoting dark
literature and the authors who work in this genre.
The organization recently launched a new literacy
partnership focusing on young adult (YA) readers.
The goal of this effort is to promote reading in
general—and horror fiction in particular.

International Arthurian Society (IAS)
North American Branch
Joseph M. Sullivan
Secretary-Treasurer
211 Castro Street
Norman, OK 73069
Web site: http://www.internationalarthuriansociety.com
The IAS is a network of people who take a scholarly
interest in literature and film centered on the leg-
ends of King Arthur. The organization was formed
in 1948 to bring together scholars from around the
world who are interested in Arthurian legends.

International Cryptozoology Museum
11 Avon Street
Portland, ME 04101
(207) 518-9496
Web site: http://cryptozoologymuseum.com

The International Cryptozoology Museum in Portland,
    Maine, has exhibits of various types of cryptids,
    including Bigfoot, Nessie, a prehistoric fish called a
    coelacanth, and the Jersey Devil. Founded by
    famed cryptozoologist Loren Coleman, this museum
    has more than three thousand items on display.

International UFO and Research Museum
114 N. Main Street
Roswell, NM 88203
(800) 822-3545
Web site: http://www.roswellufomuseum.com
The International UFO and Research Museum provides
    information about UFO phenomena, including the
    famous Roswell Incident of 1947, crop circles,
    UFO sightings, Area 51, ancient astronauts, and
    alien abductions. The museum also serves as a
    center for researchers, authors, students, and
    others looking for information on UFOs.

Mystery Writers of America (MWA)
1140 Broadway, Suite 1507
New York, NY 10001
(212) 888-8171
Web site: http://www.mysterywriters.org
The Mystery Writers of America is an organization for
    mystery and crime writers, aspiring crime writers,
    and anyone who likes to read mysteries and crime
    fiction. The organization sponsors the Helen
    McCloy Scholarship to help aspiring mystery
    writers improve their craft.

Science Fiction and Fantasy Writers of America (SFWA)
P.O. Box 3238
Enfield, CT 06083-3238
Web site: http://www.sfwa.org
The Science Fiction and Fantasy Writers of America is
an organization for authors of science fiction,
fantasy, and related genres. Past and present
members include Isaac Asimov, Anne McCaffrey,
Ray Bradbury, and Andre Norton.

Society of Children's Book Writers & Illustrators (SCBWI)
8271 Beverly Boulevard
Los Angeles, CA 90048
(323) 782-1010
Web site: http://www.scbwi.org
The Society of Children's Book Writers & Illustrators is
an organization for writers and illustrators of
children's and young adult literature. The group
has chapters around the world where members
can share ideas, information, and tips about
writing children's literature.

WEB SITES

Due to the changing nature of Internet links, Rosen
Publishing has developed an online list of Web sites
related to the subject of this book. This site is updated
regularly. Please use this link to access the list:

http://www.rosenlinks.com/AAA/yancey

Bray, Libba. *The Diviners*. New York, NY: Little, Brown Books for Young Readers, 2012.

Brooks, Terry. *Armageddon's Children*. New York, NY: Del Rey, 2006.

Brooks, Terry. *The Sword of Shannara*. New York, NY: Ballantine Books, 1977.

Castellucci, Cecil. *First Day on Earth*. New York, NY: Scholastic Press, 2011.

Clarke, Arthur C. *2001: A Space Odyssey*. New York, NY: New American Library, 1968.

Dahl, Roald. *Charlie and the Chocolate Factory*. New York, NY: Alfred A. Knopf, 1964.

Dahl, Roald. *James and the Giant Peach*. New York, NY: Alfred A. Knopf, 1961.

Doyle, Arthur Conan. *The Original Illustrated Sherlock Holmes*. New York, NY: Castle Books, 1976.

Jinks, Catherine. *The Abused Werewolf Rescue Group*. Boston, MA: Harcourt Children's Books, 2011.

Lu, Marie. *Legend*. New York, NY: Putnam Juvenile, 2011.

McHugh, Jessica. *Rabbits in the Garden*. Cincinnati, OH: Post Mortem Press, 2011.

McNamee, Graham. *Beyond: A Ghost Story*. New York, NY: Wendy Lamb Books, 2012.

McNamee, Graham. *Bonechiller*. New York, NY: Wendy Lamb Books, 2008.

Patterson, James. *The Dangerous Days of Daniel X*. New York, NY: Little, Brown and Company, 2010.

Patterson, James. *Daniel X: Game Over*. New York, NY: Little, Brown and Company, 2011.

FOR FURTHER READING

Revis, Beth. *Across the Universe*. New York, NY: Razorbill, 2011.

Roth, Veronica. *Divergent*. New York, NY: Katherine Tegen Books, 2012.

Roth, Veronica. *Insurgent*. New York, NY: Katherine Tegen Books, 2012.

Sachar, Louis. *Holes*. New York, NY: Farrar, Straus and Giroux, 2008.

Shelly, Mary W. *Frankenstein*. New York, NY: Caxton House, 1950.

Tolkien, J. R. R. *The Hobbit*. New York, NY: Houghton Mifflin Books, 1966.

Zusak, Markus. *The Book Thief*. New York, NY: Knopf Books for Young Readers, 2006.

Bloomsbury Children's Publishing. "A Conversation with Rick Yancey, Author of *The Extraordinary Adventures of Alfred Kropp*." October 2005. Retrieved January 10, 2013 (http://media .bloomsbury.com/rep/files/alfredkroppauthor.pdf).

BookBrowse.com. "Richard (Rick) Yancey—An Interview with Author." Retrieved January 13, 2013 (http://www.bookbrowse.com/author _interviews/full/index.cfm/author_number/1227 /richard-rick-yancey).

Corbett, Sue. "Children's Bookshelf Talks with Rick Yancey." *Publishers Weekly*, April 5, 2007. Retrieved January 10, 2013 (http://www .publishersweekly.com/pw/by-topic/authors/ interviews/article/3039-children-s-bookshelf-talks -with-rick-yancey.html).

Deahl, Rachel. "Deals: Week of March 5, 2012." *Publishers Weekly*, March 5, 2012. Retrieved January 10, 2013 (http://www.publishersweekly .com/pw/by-topic/industry-news/book-deals /article/50930-deals-week-of-march-5-2012.html).

Dinkova, Lidia. "Local Author Ventures Into the Realm of Monsters." *Gainesville Sun*, September 22, 2009. Retrieved January 10, 2013 (http://www.gainesville .com/article/20090922/ARTICLES/909229956 ?Title=Local-author-ventures-into-the-realm-of -monsters).

DreadCentral.com. "Exclusive: Rick Yancey Talks *The Monstrumologist*, *The Curse of the Wendigo*, and More." December 1, 2010. Retrieved January 12,

2013 (http://www.dreadcentral.com/news/41214
/exclusive-rick-yancey-talks-monstrumologist
-curse-wendigo-and-more).

Ehrenfeld, Tom. "Q&A with Rick Yancey—Taxes, Drama,
and Honor." 800 CEO READ, April 17, 2006.
Retrieved January 12, 2013 (http://blog
.800ceoread.com/2006/04/17/qa-with-rick
-yancey-taxes-drama-and-honor).

Fickley-Baker, Jennifer. "Lakeland High Grad Writes a
Monster of a Novel." TheLedger.com, September
15, 2009. Retrieved January 15, 2013 (http://
www.theledger.com/article/20090915/NEWS
/909155017?p=all&tc=pgall).

GoodReads.com. "Interview with Richard Yancey."
October 2009. Retrieved January 15, 2013
(http://www.goodreads.com/interviews/show
/251.Rick_Yancey).

Hendrick, Katie. "5 Questions with Local Author Rick
Yancey." *Gainesville Sun*, January 21, 2007.
Retrieved January 14, 2013 (http://www
.gainesville.com/article/20070121/DAYBREAK
/70121015?p=all&tc=pgall).

Jace, E. F. "Writer to Writer: Rick Yancey." *Verbose
Veracity* (blog), June 24, 2012. Retrieved January
20, 2013 (http://efjace.wordpress.com/2012/06
/24/writer-to-writer-rick-yancey/).

Lodge, Sally. "Putnam Rolls Out Cover of Yancey's 'The
5th Wave.'" *Publishers Weekly*, November 1,
2012. Retrieved January 18, 2013 (http://www
.publishersweekly.com/pw/by-topic/childrens

/childrens-book-news/article/54576-putnam-rolls
-out-cover-of-yancey-s-the-5th-wave.html).

Mahoney, Vivian Lee. "WBBT: An Interview with Rick
Yancey." VivianLeeMahoney.com, November 7,
2007. Retrieved January 10, 2013 (http://www
.vivianleemahoney.com/2007/11/07/wbbt-an
-interview-with-rick-yancey).

MonsterLibrarian.com. "Interview with Rick Yancey."
September 2009. Retrieved January 12, 2013
(http://monsterlibrarian.com/interviews.htm
#Interview_with_Rick_Yancey).

Neely, Jack. "The Highly Effective Novelist: Suddenly
Prolific Author Richard Yancey Talks About His
Creation, Knoxville-Based Would-Be Detective
Teddy Ruzak." MetroPulse.com, July 2, 2008.
Retrieved January 11, 2013 (http://www
.metropulse.com/news/2008/jul/02/highly
-effective-novelist/?print=1).

Olson, Kari. "Author Interview Rick Yancey." *A Good
Addiction* (blog), November 23, 2009. Retrieved
January 11, 2013 (http://agoodaddiction
.blogspot.com/2009/11/author-interview-rick
-yancey.html).

Orange County Library System. "Meet the Author: Rick
Yancey." YouTube.com, June 1, 2007. Retrieved
January 15, 2013 (http://www.youtube.com
/watch?v=_LlfeyqTfAc).

Quinn, Celeste. "*Confessions of a Tax Collector: One
Man's Tour of Duty Inside the IRS*." WILL Radio,
December 20, 2004. Retrieved January 15, 2013

(http://will.illinois.edu/afternoonmagazine
/interview/aftmag041220/).

Roy, Leila. "Rick Yancey, on the Monstrumology
Situation." *Bookshelves of Doom* (blog), August
16, 2011. Retrieved January 13, 2013 (http://
bookshelvesofdoom.blogs.com/bookshelves
_of_doom/2011/08/rick-yancey-on-the
-monstrumology-situation.html).

Scott, Karen S. "Talking with Award-Winning Author
Rick Yancey About *The Monstrumologist*." *Carpe
Keyboard* (blog), November 2, 2010. Retrieved
January 20, 2013 (http://carpekeyboard.blogspot
.com/2010/11/talking-with-award-winning-writer
-rick.html).

Stewart, Sarah L. "Gainesville's Rick Yancey Releases
Mystery." *Gainesville Sun*, August 27, 2006.
Retrieved January 14, 2013 (http://www
.gainesville.com/article/20060827/DAYBREAK
/208270360?Title=Gainesville-s-Rick-Yancey
-releases-mystery).

Stewart, Sarah L. "Inventing Alfred." *Gainesville Sun*,
December 10, 2005. Retrieved January 14, 2013
(http://www.gainesville.com/article/20051210
/DAYBREAK/51209041?p=all&tc=pgall).

Stewart, Sarah. "Yancey Delivers Emotionally
Charged Second Book of Alfred Kropp Series."
Gainesville Sun, May 5, 2007. Retrieved
January 14, 2013 (http://www.gainesville.com
/article/20070505/SUNFRONT/705050322
?p=all&tc=pgall).

Yancey, Richard. *Confessions of a Tax Collector: One Man's Tour of Duty Inside the IRS*. New York, NY: HarperCollins, 2004.

Yancey, Richard. "How a Tax Collector Became a Novelist: A Highly Effective Tale of Love." *Gainesville Magazine*, December 4, 2006. Retrieved January 14, 2013 (http://www .gainesville.com/article/20061204/MAGAZINE11 /61203047?p=all&tc=pgall).

ABOUT THE AUTHOR

Lisa Wade McCormick is an award-winning writer and investigative reporter. She has also written eighteen nonfiction books for children. Lisa and her family live in Kansas City, Missouri. She often visits schools and libraries with her golden retriever, who is a Reading Education Assistance Dog (R.E.A.D.). The goal of the R.E.A.D. program is to improve children's literacy skills by giving them the opportunity to read to specially trained therapy dogs.

PHOTO CREDITS

Cover, pp. 3, 76–77 Karen Huang; p. 7 Simon & Shuster/ Photograph courtesy of the author; pp. 10–11 State Archives of Florida; p. 14 Semmick Photo/Shutterstock .com; pp. 16–17 smart.art/Shutterstock.com; pp. 18–19 Bloomberg/Getty Images; pp. 22–23 © AP Images/San Francisco Chronicle/Christina Koci Hernandez; pp. 26–27 Walter Bibikow/Lonely Planet Images/Getty Images; p. 31 The Stapleton Collection/Art Resource, NY; p. 37 Juanmonino/E+/Getty Images; p. 41 AND Inc./Shutterstock .com; p. 43 © AP Images; p. 47 Columbia Pictures/ American Zoetrope/Ronald Grant Archive/Mary Evans/ Everett Collection; p. 51 Simon & Shuster; p. 54 Michael Courtney/Warner Bros./Getty Images; pp. 56–57 © Michel Delluc/XPN-REA/Redux; p. 59 Steve Mack/WireImage/Getty Images; pp. 66–67 a creation of samuelbradleyphotography .com/Flickr/Getty Images; p. 69 Rocket Publishing/SSPL/ Getty Images; p. 72 7831/Gamma-Rapho/Getty Images; cover and interior pages background (marbleized texture) javarman/Shutterstock.com; cover and interior pages (book) www.iStockphoto.com/Andrzej Tokarski; interior pages background (trees) © iStockphoto.com/AVTG.

Designer: Nicole Russo; Editor: Andrea Sclarow Paskoff; Photo Researcher: Karen Huang